DOE SONGS

ACKNOWLEDGEMENTS

Thank you to my husband Kevin and our beautiful son, Rafael. This book, and so much else, would not be possible without you both.

I am grateful for the support and mentorship of Pascale Petit. Thank you to the Hollick Family Charitable Trust, The Arvon Foundation, and Bocas Literary Festival. Thank you to Jeremy Poynting and Hannah Bannister for your patience over the years while this collection was still growing and becoming. To my poem-sister Shivanee Ramlochan, I am so grateful for your feedback and friendship.

Thank you to my grandmother, collector of my very first poems.

Several of these poems, or versions of them, were published in the following journals: *Prairie Schooner*, *The Rialto*, *Poetry London*, *The Cordite Review*, *Small Axe*, *Moko Caribbean Arts and Letters*, the *Literary Review*, *tongues of the ocean*, *Bim Literary Magazine* and the *Asian American Literary Review*.

DANIELLE BOODOO-FORTUNÉ

DOE SONGS

P E E P A L   T R E E

First published in Great Britain in 2018
Peepal Tree Press Ltd
17 King's Avenue
Leeds LS6 1QS
UK

ISBN 13: 978184524188

Supported using public funding by
ARTS COUNCIL
ENGLAND

CONTENTS

TO ENTER MY MOTHER'S HOUSE

The Heron god created daughter
on the last day. Not knowing
what to do with the longing
left over from creation, he poured it
into her open mouth, still warm
and echoing with earth.

To enter my mother's house
I must walk backwards with
smoke in my mouth.

To pass through the keyhole
I must become a spout
of water, a single hair
from an ocelot's back.

I must go back thirty years
to recreate myself, carve
my face on the unburnt tip
of a match, strike my teeth
thrice against her name.

The daughter is always hungry,
walking backwards through locked
doors, breaking her teeth on
teacups and unasked questions.

In my mother's house,
blue as bruise and dry
as tinder, there are rooms
I am too tall to enter.

I must make myself small
and light as a bee, suspend

myself among the dust motes
and droplets, hum and fidget
among the noiseless things.
I must not disturb the dishes
in the sink, tread softly round
the sunken bed.

If the daughter, milk-soft
and heavy with egg,
does not re-enter the house
of her mother, she will give birth
to a siege of night herons.
They will be born ravenous,
eat the heart from her body
before they can walk.

To re-enter my mother's house
I must walk backwards cloaked
in purple, the colour of hurt.

I must never ask about my birth.

HOW TO MAKE HIM STAY

Go into your garden at night
and whisper his true names.

The plants that cry out in ecstasy
will be the ones you must pick.
Cut the softest joints
with your best knife,
take the traitorous shoots
into the kitchen and drown them.

Take him apart each night
like brittle clockwork.
Then put him back together
with your teeth and nails.

Fix what you can.

Kiss every long silence, untie
the thread of each lie
then set it free.

Anything he loves
more than you
must be quieted.

DOE

The Hunter Remembers the Doe

You see, her eyes spoke
but I didn't listen.
It happened like this:
The dogs leapt,
seized her by the throat.

I pulled the trigger,
turned her face into
the damp earth
so I wouldn't see her eyes
while I did my work.

But once I drew the blade
against her side, I knew.

It was still warm, breathing
deep inside the half-moon
of her open belly.
"Leave it", someone said,
But I couldn't. I feared
the darkness would swallow me,
that the sighing trees
would remember my face.
It blinked twice beneath
its caul of wet silk, looked
right into my blindness
with eyes that spoke
the same language
as its mother's.

The Hunter's Wife Remembers the Fawn

When he brought me the fawn
that Sunday evening,
its weight in my arms
felt somehow like prayer.

Its eyes were like yours,
difficult, hungry,
heavy with the memory
of its mother's ruined body.

But the truth is,
it was you who broke my heart
that night, you with your small hands
made for holding on too long.
You didn't even make a sound
when, startled by its aloneness,
the fawn thrashed and split
its skull on the kitchen floor.

The Hunter's Only Daughter Hears the Fawn Song

There is music in the forest,
a word I heard the bush tell.

It is a single sound,
a song for the barefoot
and the aching of heart.

They say once you hear it,
you shed your old tongue
and learn to speak
in the soft whoop
of the lonely.

They say once you hear it,
you lay yourself down
beneath the trees,

and the fawn is the one
walking home
in your skin.

DREAM OF MY DAUGHTER AS A FAWN

When she pauses in the clearing between cedars
slender neck arched like a drawn bow,
I want to kneel, hold her against my thundering heart,
love her into tameness, but I know I cannot.
Her amber eyes are her father's, but her wildness is mine.
January rain comes, stirring the mountain's quiet,
washing small cloven prints from the forest floor.
Back home, the bed must be still warm from her body
covered with the soft down of her baby coat.
Such spaces we have built for her, rooms furnished
with tenderness, each brick laid with love.
See my hooves, mother, she whispers. The beginnings
of my antlers. See how I am fiercely made.
Weak sunlight casts her fur golden.
Oh, I too was a fawn once. I know
the shots fire whether we are wild or not.
The hunters come with their guns
even though we are good.
Go on and run, I whisper
and her soft hooves fly.

DREAM OF MY DAUGHTER AS A TURTLE

Two years ago, I begged the goddess of the gulf
to take me safely to shore. On the crest
of a smashed wave, a leatherback thrashed
in a tangle of nets.

I have always been afraid of the ocean.
Now, in her presence, I grow fins
and a longing for the churning blue.

Deep inside the dream where
I am the mother of a thousand turtles,
she stirs, the ocean floods my
just-waking mouth.

TAYRA

We brought them in from the mainland,
that body of earth we have no memory of
but whose violent three-mouthed sighing
reminds us of the beasts we half-were.

Unlike the birds and the great cats,
this one raged at the churning sea,
drew blood through wet burlap
with arrowhead teeth.

The others I sold, but this one I loved
because she would not be tamed.

Tayra daughter, chien bois,
little goddess of the high woods,
I have taken the forest from you
and given you the safety of walls.

I no longer take to the sea.
My fierce love for you has ruined me
for the capture of beasts. My heart
has grown soft like the spaces
in between your small paws.

Before bed, I brush the burrs and wings
from your dark hair, file your teeth
and nails to sharp points, feed you a paste
made from crushed fruit and moths.

Still, every morning the house
is filled with the musk
of your hatred
for me.

To atone for what I have taken,
I offer you my protection and
the notched flute of my throat.

Each night I lie awake.
I keep watch over my daughter, the one
hunters will learn to fear most.

PORTRAIT OF MY FATHER AS A GROUPER

The weight is too much to carry, even underwater.

You lie in a bed of silt and algae,
wait for the lord of sunken things
to call your name and raise you home.

When I come to see you, I forget how to breathe.
There is ash on your forehead, your silver mouth
cracked with thirst and too much salt.

Here is no place for the living.
In the cot beside you lies a hollowed eel,
still sparking faintly with the charge
of what was.

Barred windows keep out an unchanging sea,
but all the doors here are broken.
You say there have been gunshots
in the ward next door, that the drowning
cry out at night for mercy, young men caught
between teeth, old men tangled in nets.

I show you photos of what my life looks like.
I have chosen only the bright things,
left out the spiny years of pain. Oh, Father,
look at the face you have given me to live with.

You have pulled our lives,
soft and impermanent as polyps,
into your crushing mouth,
but as you once were, I am a fish unwilling to drown.

So I sit at your undersea bedside as you pray,
and I wait,
boning knife clutched in hands
in case your god does not come.

HOWLER

Even if you never wake
inside this flute of light
this whip of green, whistling
the first god's riverine
alleluia,

there still must be
the need to howl.

You feel it on mornings
in the taxi's damp chest.
It starts beneath your feet,
humming thread of need
rising up your spine.

Behind the glass now, you are
a creature dull-eyed and
crookedly tamed.

Here is no land
for wild beasts;

let the silver cross
round your neck and
the blade in your waistband
bear witness.

So what is there to do
with the surging flood
of this day

but to turn your throat into
a gourd that must hold it?

Even you must know this:
everything that breathes
will howl.

FEATHERS

While he hunts
birds, she sews them from
burlap and lace. For years
I've been drawing her
heart-shaped face.
We both try to
remake what
we cannot
save

GUAYABA

There is no sugar
to be found in San Felipe.
With two hours to kill, we drink guayaba
juice, compare names of gods and fruits.

The world ends and begins anew
a thousand times over
breakfast.

TANGERINES

The bus has broken down miles from Barquisimeto.
I am stranded in the hot yard of my heart's third chamber,
her name springing from my mouth
in the language of water.

The translator, whose name resembles air, says
we are standing in the dark
between the map's known places.

She does not know here.

Here is a pause
between mountains, streets
ablaze with red dust and tangerines.

At home, the ground my mother plants
will yield no sweetness.
It is veined with too much water.
She presses a boot to the earth, the roots weep.

Last year, we picked an acre of barren white citrus,
sliced them open, squeezed the stringy flesh
in search of fragrance.

Now, a woman is leaning against a faded blue stall,
her arms full of fruit and sky.
Eight miles across the sea,
my mother is sitting alone in a field
of bachac and blank trees.

Back in Caracas, I write to you with red dust
still beneath my nails.

I want to tell you about the hours that lie between
nowhere and here, red earth, miles of bright fruit,
filling my lungs like hot daylight,

your name, that place we spent the burnt hours,
memory, those things that need no language.

If you let it, each acre will speak:
let no one name you.
Let no one claim you.
Mother, forgive me, but gather your maps
and run.

JAGUAR MARY, MARIA LIONZA

Y
our
poet
is so
young.
What can
she know
of drowned
loves and being
swallowed alive
by a vengeful
god
?

If
you
do not
fight in
side of the
beast's belly,
time will turn
you both into
mountains
and if
you
see
your own
face in the
rearview mirror
shut your eyes.
Sorte is still
so very

| Jaguar | *clos* | Mary |
| I have | *e* | always |

25

                  longed   to hold
                      a god   by the
                          hipbones.
                          Mother,
          P   pray for   at
          oeta,   me   bay.
        wear this   .   When you
      necklace of red   come back here
    rosary peas, of jumbie   the rains will be start-
  beads to keep your beasts   ing. Bring your best bones.

BOA GRAVIDA

When we were new,
our love still minnow-soft
and silver, you set their names
like nets along the water's edge.

Now the first, a son,
surfaces, a great fish writhing
in the basket of my hips.

These last gravid days of rain
we digest the remains of years.

You speak of everything to come,
how you long to cradle the lotus-bud
of his skull in the broad leaf of your hand,
to swim in with him from the other side.

Until then, let us wait here in the restless earth,
whisper to each other in mangrove tongues.

Tell me I am beautiful and cold.
I will tell you how thirsty I am
for a mouthful of light.

At night I ache. Veins purple and rise
with this sudden season of blood.
Pelvic plates shift, bones shudder.

I am the great mother boa
turning the soft egg of the world
beneath my ribs. I will tear myself in two
and heal before morning.

MAMA RIVER

This river is not my mother.

My mother is the red knot in my eye

My mother is this necklace of beads and bone

My mother is lichen, moss and undergrowth

My mother is salt, tide and undertow

My mother is an unstitched tear, an echo chamber

My mother is the place where my son is not

My mother is the absence of my father

She is named in the image of God.

CORNBIRD

Cornbird
knows when
storm is coming.
She reads the sky's
fat blue script, feels
salt blades on morning
breeze. The tree has been
standing for many lifetimes
so she must trust its deep roots.
Hers are not the first young to sway
in the wind, hammocked in a nest woven fine
and heavy as jeweller's wire. At last light she clings
from treetops and warbles her love, yellow and true.
My newborn sleeps through the fevered August rain,
lulled by its warmth and insistence. It lasts days.
At night we cannot tell thunder
from gunfire

SOMBRA

The dove's throat is the valley
of the shadow, light breaking
in the east, first songs of mourning.

Then it comes, bright chorus
of frenzied wings, clearly now
the penumbra of your passing
fanned wide across the small world.

We are left with this knowing,
bitter smoke, oil and musk,
grief and crushed flowers.

I am a thing made of bolts,
hinges and unburnable wood –
my body fashioned into a bridge
between water and fire,
his presence and your leaving.

Although you are gone,
he is stirring with the sun,
lifting his new heart up
into the first light.

If grief is bitter smoke,
the sting of ash
at the back of the throat,
then joy is a taste of honey,
warm rainwater, the quickening
of sugar on the tongue.

My mourning dove's heart
must find a way
to hold both.

Oh, Grandfather,
will you know each other
in the way that roots reach out,
dreaming in the earth's deep sleep,
or meet in the middle of the bridge,
the endless, the *sombra*, resting space
between shadows?

THE FIFTH MONTH

The fifth month my body splits
like a fallen seed pod.

It is too early for this.
I am barefaced and unprepared
as an island,

my fear sudden and tidal.

To keep you, I shrink
so that God will not find me.

I hide my heart
in the birdseed and the boiling-pots.

I let them bind my insides
with wire and thread.

Your father hacks off
two years of his hair.

We name you, unname you,
then name you again.

No sign must appear
but the whorled seashell
of your forming spine,

no sound but the dull hoofbeat
of your small heart.

AMATEUR MIDWIFERY

For a smooth delivery
eat dasheen bush in the morning.
Boil without salt. Add coconut milk if you like,
but the greener the better.

Eat as much ochro as you can stand;
the baby will slip right out.

Drown everything in oil:
food, skin, hair.

Drink lots of water;
leave glasses around the house
so you won't forget.

Choose your fruit carefully;
look out for strange markings.

Don't watch the news.

Wear blue to keep
bad spirits off.

Get lots of sleep.

Walk often.

Try not to sleepwalk.

Eat enough fish.

Grow gills.

Pray.

Try not to believe
everything you read.

THE LABOURING MAMMAL'S JOURNAL OF HOURS

The new mother is the site
of a thousand beginnings,
          In the beginning was the first cry melting in air, holy and new
an entirely new creature
patched together cervix to sternum
with catgut and frayed stamens,
hot wolf's breath bursting
the unlit cave of her chest.
                     and before this, the silent science of bonemaking

               This wave is muscle turning,
               this wave is bone opening. This wave
               is where you end and another begins.

       (If I can no longer write, then
       you must retrieve the brackets
       of my spine when it is finished.)

Beasts like me keep third and fourth sets of teeth for just this reason.
Easier to gnash, better to howl with.

We do not cry out.
We count the waves in strange markings.
We give birth to fearless young.
We eat the afterbirth
                    O green god, first mother,
                    she who made the water,
                    lay your hands on me
                    shake the firmament
                    of my body,
                    deliver me from doubt.

DELIVERY

perhaps
it is still night
time breaks
in half, struck
down by
your cry
whose body
is this?

someone else's
legs
sugar
in the mouth
to keep from
fainting
rough cloth
rainstorm

need of warmth
curving needles
someone else's
blood
your breath
steaming red
my arms
the sudden weight
of you

ALTERNATIVE REMEDIES

Take care of your body. Your body is home,
It is meat, it is bruise.
Hydrate, drink eight glasses a day;
the chemicals have run amok.
Television hurts your ears. The window looms before you.
A windblown umbrella breaks your heart.
Take care of your cracked tailbone,
your broken capillaries. Avoid drugs.
                              Avoid pesticides.
Most of all, you are milk,
you are scar tissue.
You are milk, you are need.

Take some time for yourself. Set back all the clocks.
        Fly backwards
into the keyhole.
Run the shower scalding hot. Disappear.

Talk about it. Take this and eat it.
This is my body. It will be given up for you.
Find me, lay beside me. I once was water.

LEARNING TO BREATHE IN LUMINOUS WATER

They say you can teach yourself
to breathe underwater here.

I've heard of women who could do it,
hold their breaths till their veins
burst their banks, flowed on until
their hearts emptied in the sea.

I go down to the river each morning,
unlace my skin, spread the twin nets
of my lungs out against these rocks.

This is the same river I was born in,
the one my grandmother gave birth in.

This is the same river that bursts,
each decade, into a million lights
and if you learn to breathe here,
your body stays forever lit
with the secret.

NOVENA FOR A WOUNDED WILD MOTHER

If he returns, I swear I will
eat my mercy. Wild beasts like
me cannot spare an ounce
of love. Better milk.
Better water.
Better meat.
Pray for
me.

O
blessed
one, must I
be mourning and
weeping this long? The
forest has turned into
a vale of tears. My cubs sate
their hunger on my loneliness,

milk teeth growing hollower each day.

O clement one, make me as strong
as the river, let me touch
the hem of your garment.
I am a mother
just like you are;
deliver
me from
doubt.

Bless
-ed is
thy fruit, but
in my mouth it
all tastes so charred and

bitter. I make this milk
from nothing but my anger.
Mother, bless each tender navel
God knows I cannot do it myself,

I have been weakened enough. Love
breaks me, stone over bone o-
ver and over again.
Tell the moon not to
call me. Tell the
cubs not to
make a
sound.

Sweet
mother
of mercy,
hold me up to
the light. My will has
been broken. Nothing grows
under my feet. The young are
always hungry, always searching

for the heart beneath my tired breasts.

I will bear no more sons. Let the
dry leaves fall. Let the waxing
moon come calling. Even
my little beasts, now
sure-footed and
free. No one
comes for
me.

O
mama
of god, leave
me. The pack will
devour me now that
I am useless, burnt and
barren as the mountain side.
Holy fire sweep me dry. Forgive
my empty belly. Forgive my teeth.

WAITING

i've been waiting in places you cannot begin to imagine like
under the streetlight by the corner, with slick toads
climbing down my throat, and in the hollow
below your door where you toss all
the muddy shoes, and the bed of
leafy earth at the river's end
just to see you wearing
your old seashell
smile, the day in
your voice
saying
speak

CARRYING HOME

After Adrian Villar Rojos' The Most Beautiful of All Mothers (XVI)

My love, it is December
and I am so far away from home,

from the bright new grass
of your infant breath.

The world seems weary of itself.

Each day sloughs off a pale skin
and lays its head down to rest.

It is still so strange to be empty of you.
My body is lonely, stranded

in a long field of yearning. I burst
my banks with unrequited milk,

stand cold and useless as a statue.

I gather these words to take them with me,
home weighing heavy on my back.

The weight is all that keeps us together now.
I must manage it any way I can.

THE GARDENER'S DAUGHTER IN THE EVENING

On evenings she lies,
back pressed to the road.

Soft pitch swells beneath her heels,
the blue sky crowns her.

Somewhere, metal drags
across the soil's hot heart;
men's voices crackle in the distance
like burning grass.

There is nowhere to hurry to,
no circle of lonely earth
to set down the halved
seed of her name.

Here is both home
and nowhere.

The world beyond her fingertips
stretches sharp and green
into the sun.

THE GARDENER'S DAUGHTER WRITES HOME

Listen,
ghosts don't always need
to bloom up from bones here
and it is not so simple to bury a memory.
Something always grows:
a yellow house, a shock of lilies,
a grieving daughter in a gown
of thorns.

See, I cannot plant a thing
without flinching.
Each spinning leaf, each burnt-out root
is a body in mourning.
Remember the girl, younger than I was,
who could not tell you whether
she had been beaten or loved?
You cried that night.
Even you run into the forest
when it is too much to bear.

THE GARDENER'S DAUGHTER WALKS IN THE DARK

Seven is when the blindness comes.

The dead trees hiss, spit dry heat
into the thickening night. My body
cannot hold this heat, this absence
of light.

I think of you on evenings like this.
I wonder if there was ever a wildness
that bloomed its way into your
careful heart.

I wonder if love ever blinded you.

At seven, the earth is hot and needy.
I unclasp my necklace of flies, go walking
among the untame trees to find you.

SOLAR ECLIPSE, GUAPO BEACH

The road here is imperfect geometry
spiralling round muddy hearts
of rice fern and cane flowers,
then stretching straight into the blinding sea.
Sun, startled to find moon in its eye,
blinks twice, glares across an expanse
of eager water. The flat, shuddering
pane between island and mainland
is baptised with light,
inlets and estuaries oiled with gold.

My infant son wants to kiss the face of the ocean,
brings his lips to the brim of its dazzling bowl.
He does not yet know his lungs, still longs
for the quiet and weightlessness of water,
the dull roar of heartbeat and tide.
I pour rivulets into his open hands,
touch the curls on his temples
with sea salt and light in the name
of sun and moon and holy ocean.

"Turn away from the sun," my grandmother warned,
but the day draws me, waist-deep waves pulling
the roots and fibres of my body toward
that great yellow eye. In the shadow of my chest
baby is as lithe and slick as a fish,
splashing openmouthed with terror and glee.

By the time evening spreads its fingers
across mangrove and sand, he is warm
in my arms, heavy with sleep.
The moon, miraculously unharmed
floats free, freshly rinsed and silver-white,
into a waiting sky sucked clean of light.

BRASSO, HOMEWARD

Your father was felled by a giant teak
one purple morning, in the damp
of the forest's aching mouth.

Your mother hears it a mountain away,
a rush of air sweeping from his lungs,
last, broken, holy offering of her name.

The house, now wild with her grief,
grows fibrous roots. Each empty room
smells deep and sharp as ginger.

After the burying,
your aunts undress you, show you
which roots to cut and which to keep.

They make you wash the forest
from your hands and eyes, teach you
their hymns in shrill tongues of birds.

But even now, on the Blanchisseuse road,
the trees still whisper to you
like lovers.

The cry of the bellbird
is your mother's strange keening,
and all the fallen logs,

their names long forgotten,
are your father's arms
waiting to bear you home.

THE BLUE HOUSE

The only thing I have
is my face.
Everything else is lore,
grey-blue, deep-furrowed,
tossed in the gust
of each telling.
I walk the shore, sift words
from the surf with my footprints.
One of the boats here is as blue
as my great-grandmother's house
on the hill. Her name is sea glass,
in my memory, smooth, cool
and unknowable.
A boy with my bones
walks past me, a boat's old engine
perched on his shoulder
like a great rusted gull.
We pass without speaking,
ghosts in each other's history.
I kneel, roll shells between my fingers,
chant litanies of names,
but nothing comes to me.
Nothing lasts here
but the murmur of the sea.

READER, BEWARE

For Shivanee Ramlochan

The poet is a flambeau.
The poet is a cutlass, a spear whittled
from the tallest cedar, sharpened to a fine point.
The poet cuts you without you even knowing it.
Yes, you are hurt, but my God, it is beautiful.
You are tumbling outside yourself in wet handfuls now.
Nothing will hold. A field of cedar springs up
in the yawning where you once stood.

Why are you in tears?

The poems are hard to read
and it is even harder to breathe. Something burns
the back of your eyes, tickles your throat.
Someone offers you food, offers you wine
but you have no stomach for it.
The poem wants to find you hungry, hollow
trembling inside your good shoes.

You might already be gone.

You might have left the reading some time ago,
but can't really be sure.
Nothing looks familiar except the poet's red dress.
It holds you steady in the dark room like a high pitch-oil flame.
You leave the reading, walking behind yourself
alone in the streetlight, dissolving in your own shadow.
Reader, trust me when I tell you:
only the haunting remains.

CHAMELEON THOUGHTS

I

I wear this chameleon around my neck
to keep myself from changing.
I go from fire to fire
with each new skin,
spin prophecy,
secrete visions,
shed my face again
with the turning of the moon.
This last incarnation
must not kill me yet.
I have a little luck
left.

II

I bought the chameleon pendant
from a man at Store Bay who
promised it was lucky.
I bought it on a morning when
I wasn't quite sure who I
was trying to be,
found it underneath
one massive shark tooth,
stone phallus on a string
and rough clay terrapin.
The chameleon, trapped
on flat brown medallion,
could not change
as he wanted to
and at the moment
neither could I.

III

We fear chameleons too much,
want things to be just as they seem,
we, who sell raw heart meat
to strangers, burn bridges, use
God's name without permission,
we want our small dragons
to stay green, pocket-sized,
always crushable in good conscience.

IV

Like a good chameleon,
I change when my skin
tastes danger.
Right now, I am not the one
you wanted. I am a shade alien,
I climb poisonous trees,
turn my open mouth
to the breeze.
I am not the one you
hoped to find when
you hatched me.
Perhaps you wanted
something softer, like
a bird or a butterfly.
But here I am: telescopic
eyes and all, lizard
waiting for wings
under the trees'
leaving.

V

I don't know if this pendant
will withstand the water,
but I wear it anyway.
In the hollow
of my collarbone
it rests, warm
brown stone,
for the moment
unchanging
like me
until I decide
to turn
again.

YOUR DAUGHTER IS TROUBLE

Your daughter is trouble
too much of her father's
madness in her broad bones,
too much silence in her speech,
too much wanting.
And she is only half-pretty,
ten pounds too heavy,
something sitting wild
in the ring
of her laughter.
There is a lit fuse
in your daughter's mouth,
her brownish body a bomb
set down, soft and waiting
to make war with your name.

PICTURES

I
I spent a childhood wondering
if this is what love might look like:
a pair of scorched eyes
in a hollowed-out face,
body trapped in a stifling
whirl of white.

II
The picture has been cut
into the exact size and shape
of the things he broke.
Her mouth is tight
with the strain
of smiling.
I can just make out
the colour of his sleeve,
the shadow
of his hand
across her cheek.

III
In the picture I am shapeless, soft
mouth wet and creased like a puppy's.
My mother's face is a button
unravelled and lost.
Her legs in jean shorts
are unfamiliar,
equine and spare.
Her back is curved
like a drawn bow,
and I am the small,
stepped-on creature
in the centre.

MOTHER IN THE MORNING

Mother sips tea in her garden on mornings,
abandoning the kitchen that echoes with breakfast,
lunch kits, laces untied, and the dripping faucet.
She sits on a cracked footstool in silence
as the heat from the teacup rises,
whispers warm, comforting secrets
only she can understand.

There are sharp things in the ground
and her hands are soft
but she never wears gloves.
She is not afraid of the damp, dark earth
with its shards of buried glass and crawling creatures.
She has planted hope,
seen it grown tall.

When my mother's hands are in the dew-damp earth
and she is fragile in the morning light,
sharp things are buried in her,
and I realize how the fluorescent kitchen light dims her,
hides the secret flower she is growing
that only blooms when she does.

THE VISITOR

On mornings, you bathe dust
from dust with wounded hands,
polish a memory gone dull
beneath the same rags.

The shut room holds a white bird
trapped for forgiveness' sake,
its wings unused and soft.

Who is this visitor you wait for,
the strange voice clawing its way
up the tunnel of your throat?

What incantations howled low
into the brittle cup of your palms
will comfort you?

You wait, lips tightening across teeth,
for the sound of footsteps at the door.

On evenings, your damp lights flicker
when no one comes calling.

CORONARY I

After all, you only live as long
as the cells in the umbilicus say.
You are the seedling
in your grandmother's marrow,
and you've grown accustomed to waiting,
reliving the almost-end,
the second, third
and thousandth-to-last days.
Moths burrow into flour, bread pales
and mottles with mould. This life
you have kneaded till bearable,
rolled thinner and thinner each day,
now begins to taste like metal.

CORONARY II

After a while, the words
mean nothing. What
is muscle, is vein, is needle
is better than worse than…?

What can you bear

to live / not live
with?

What is this body
if not a map of punctures,
a glossary of bruises?

What is this heart,
dull, spongy and hot,
waiting too long now,
left on the windowsill,
left to dry, left empty,
left with nothing to do but tick?

CORONARY III

Chamber: bedroom, hollow, cavern, gun.
Explosion in the engine room of your chest,
fourth door on the left.
Children surround your bed, singing
as the mother of mercy is piped down your arteries
through a yardage of stent.

THE HAUNTING OF HIS NAME

The man who loves you
is nothing but a ghost.

He walks through walls,
his name on your mouth like prayer.
His name is what you tell yourself
before you sleep, a short cry
in the stalk of your throat.

You keep him in the high slant
of your daughter's bones,
in the sheaves of guilt
tucked beneath your breasts.
Rainy mornings, you wake,
his rough hands rummaging
beneath your collarbone
for what's left of your heart.

You clothe yourself in penitence,
wear your hair shorn,
weapons in your mouth
sharp and pointed.
You must not love him,
so you bind yourself
with hunger and smoke,
sing hard against
your body's silence.

But he will not leave you,
keeps slipping through
your locked doors,
stealing the sound
from your mouth
before you speak.

The man who loves you
is a ghost to be washed
from the temple of your heart.

You must go into yourself now
with your one small flame,
burn down the haunting
of his name.

LETTERS FROM NEW GRACE

I

Daughter,
be wary of men.

They burn soliloquies,
sift charred words
through teeth.
Even their sweetest words
are bitter, melt dark
in your belly, ride
your chest like untamed
horses at daybreak.

See, I've been waiting here
since it ended, combing
the late streets for lost dogs
and scraps of your laughter.

Each day I wash
my eyes
with your memory,

Oh love,
you've been lonelier
than I can bear.

Tomorrow I will come for you,
fists oiled and hunger
strapped to my back.

Wait for me,
guard your heart
till you hear my cry.

II

Ashes anoint each rooftop;
each footstep is ground glass.

I wonder how you've managed
to outrun the decades of loss.

Dying light frames your shoulders,
the tight angle of your martyr's spine.

We were worlds from here,
once.

The skyline is a hatchwork of bones
eaten clean and left behind,

but we are too hungry here
to make memory.

Your eyes billow with smoke in the ruined room.
New Grace was never home, you say.

Home is for the next life.
Here is already burnt.

III

There are no more stars, Mother.
No light but the glare
of the moon's white grin.

I've no words left to write,
nothing to say but this:

Over time, one forgets
the business of bodies.

I carry my bones softly,
bear his weight while
I count the ceiling's rotted ribs.

A tree still lives here,
somehow.

When I breathe deep,
something yellow, ambrosial
swells in me like
the distant memory of love.

But nothing bears.

God, I am tired of being young
upon this dead earth.
I am so tired of being
someone's daughter.

LAST POSTCARD FROM NEW GRACE

The nets drowned my mother's great heart
long before I learned to weep.
My father, a fisherman's son, wore his hair
slicked back, razored at the temples
to keep the vultures away.

My brother said Daddy's left eye
once belonged to a fearsome fish.

I'd often wondered about
the crown of bones
on the dresser,

but there are no corners
left here
for hiding things.

I keep my mother's picture
tucked beneath my waistband,
against the stitched muscle
of my belly.

My right eye is a sharpened blade,
my breasts are bound by
the ribs of fearsome fish.

There is no mercy left for daughters
in New Grace.

ON BEING BURNT

The burning starts with a word,
a struck match,
a searing fist.

You lie still.
You are so tired
of struggling

and there is no one waiting
to beat down the door
and save you from burning
inside your own body.

Someone once told you
that love must be borne
tight against your breasts
like an orphaned thing,
a calcified child.

You've been carrying yours
like this, all these years…
swaddled in sheets,
pressed up hard
against your lungs.

Still, you've always known
that the wild thing
would not be satisfied
with bread alone,

that one day
it would hear
your heart's thin shriek
beneath all the flammable layers
of cotton and skin,

that the thing
you brought to your bed
would burn you.

And now, nothing is left
of your eaten self
but smoke, rising
from the house
never yours
to begin with.

In the bushes
something picks your hair
from its teeth,
walks upright
towards some other death.

THE NINTH MOON

i count
nine moons around
the world you promised
me, eight of them luminous
one dark, covered
with ice

PRAISE SONG IN CARBON

All forests burn, and all bodies.
Under each taut surface
arteries of fire,

hills in dry season, old letters
of confession, pyres on the riverbank
wick of your baptismal candle:

all that was done can be burnt.

Now abandon your four walls
and ceiling of flame,
what's gone is gone.

O eternal thumbprint, smudge
of coal, sacred ash,
now we are clean as a field razed by fire,
clean as God's first atom.

A POEM ON THE WORLD'S LAST NIGHT

It is late now, and I am tired
of the same streets and the same
strangers, mute as bottles.

I am tired of walking home with
a throat full of noise and glass,
my body clutched trembling
and closed.

I am weary of the pinned smile
and bound breasts, the silent women
with eyes like rainstorms, nursing
buttoned-up hurricane hearts.

It is late, and I am tired
of sweeping brimstone
beneath the bed,
pretending fires don't start
in quiet rooms.

So if this is what remains
of the world's last night,
who will stop me from burning
down my burglarproof bones,

from breaking the windows
and falling headfirst into
the moon's blue end?

BOOK OF NIGHTS

I

You are standing at the window
broken,
picking glass stars
from your wet mouth.
You've kept nothing of his
but the unbelieving children
and a faint memory
of shifting bones.
But some nights,
the moon's hard eye holds you
closer, tighter
than your body can bear.
You open your book of nights,
unreadable and faded.

II

He's been warned
of her sharp white teeth,
the necklace of vertebrae kept
hidden among the underthings.

Her openmouthed kisses leave him raw,
his throat lined with salt.

She is too hungry to be trusted.

Tonight, while she sleeps,
he will fill his heart with stones,
drown it deep.

III

Sleep is not the forgetting it used to be.

You put the kettle on, wash your face,
watch fireflies crawl on the ceiling
till day breaks.
Love has locked you in this body,
fashioned your wings into tired hands
that fall open, suppliant,
on his chest
like dead spiders.

IV

Mine is a magician's smile
styled with mirrors and smoke,
red wax scrawl, trick of the eye.

At night, when my skin is bare,
I am little more than a question.
I lie still, wait for the one who
will happen upon my true face.

When touched too gently, I say things
only trees understand.

A HAMMER TO LOVE WITH

On her sixteenth birthday
you gave her a hammer,
told her,
Here, love with this.

Love has been hard
since then, and brittle.

You've gone ten years
without sleep, five years
without silence.

Today she lets you in,
mines the cracks in her bones
with the point
of her tongue
and listens.

You straighten the sheets, crush
fennel seeds in her tea
to keep the gods at bay.
How any man can survive her
is beyond your wisdom, but
in some way you are proud
of the thing she's become.

When did it happen,

she asks, as she always will,
her tongue bruised
from the night's work.

When did it start?

You remember, oh yes.
She must've been seventeen,
dragged him home bleeding from the mouth
and singing in god's tongue,
between her bone-sharp teeth,
the hammer, dark and glistening.

Or at least that's how you remember it.

You say nothing,
wipe the spilt marrow
from her breasts,
feed her, spoon idle talk
into her bitten mouth.

You do what you can.

Oh, this one is difficult;
you can tell by her eyes.
She is afraid he might undo her,
take her by the hips
too gently,

undress
the wound

too slowly.

But you smell the bones
buried shallow in the bed.
She will manage him,
like she always does.
There is no tenderness
here, not since
then.

Tonight you will comfort yourself
with smoke and prayer.
When she licks her way
into him, you will wish
you hadn't heard the cry,

wish you hadn't said the words.

But it is finished, you tell yourself.
And it is not your doing.
After all, a heart too soft
will fail, collapse in the lung,
send you fumbling for a body
to breathe for you.

You know this better than most.

After all,
anything swung hard enough
will kill a man,
hammer and heart alike.

FIVE SONGS FOR PETRA

I

They say my great-grandmother was mad,
but I like to think she flew into herself,
got trapped in her feline heart
and decided to stay there.

II

He was already married when he met her.
Her name juts from the borders of his own,
half-Carib woman with a forest in her bones,
mother of his mad children, she who would dare,
with her sharp white teeth, to try and eat him alive.

III

They say my great-grandmother lived alone in the leaning house.
I slept there once, long after her death,
my body rocked between the walls by
a slow August earthquake.
I smelled her in the damp floorboards.
The syllables of her name
rolled through the broken windows like
swollen fruit and grating metal.

That was how I found her.

IV

He was already married when he met her,
but there was something about her
that caught him, pierced his skin.

Her love was an unsheathed claw.

He waited, tunnelled around in the flute
of her hip to find the sound
of himself.

But soon, the beasts around the bed
would not let him in. The house bulged
with books and bared teeth.

When she began to sing to the trees,
he decided it would be best
to remain whole.

V

There is a door that leads
down a broken hill. Trees grow there,
but are dark, burdened with moss
and too much hunger.
If she walked here with her dogs,
barefoot and half-blind, then
I might still find her.

If I go mad, like she did,
I wonder if you will stay.

ABOUT THE AUTHOR

Danielle Boodoo-Fortuné is a poet and artist from Trinidad & Tobago. Her writing and art have appeared in several local and international journals such as *Bim: Arts for the 21st Century*, *The Caribbean Writer*, *Small Axe Literary Salon*, *Poui: Cave Hill Journal of Creative Writing*, *Anthurium: A Caribbean Studies Journal*, *Dirtcakes Journal*, *Blackberry: A Magazine*, *Room Magazine* and others.

Danielle was awarded The Charlotte and Isidor Paiewonsky Prize by the Caribbean Writer's editorial board in 2009, nominated for a Pushcart Prize in 2010, and awarded the Small Axe Poetry Prize in 2012. In 2013, she was nominated for Best New Poets and shortlisted for the Wasafiri New Writing Prize, as well as the Montreal Poetry Prize. In 2015 she won the Hollick Arvon Caribbean Writers Prize and a selection of her poetry was published in *Coming Up Hot: Eight New Poets from the Caribbean* (Peekash Press, 2015). In 2016, she won the Wasafiri New Writing Prize for poetry.

In 2012, Danielle was selected for the *Urban Heartbeat Project*, a street art project that took place across the Caribbean and Central America. Her art was also featured as part of group exhibitions such as *Women Make Art* (WoMA) exhibition in Grenada. Danielle's first solo art exhibition, *Criatura*, was held at the Art Society of Trinidad and Tobago in 2013. In that year, her work was featured in group exhibitions, *Music is the Soul* in Toronto and *The Femail Project* in Birmingham, UK. In 2014, she was chosen to be part of the Museum of Latin American Art's Frida Kahlo-themed Women's Day exhibition.

MORE NEW POETRY FROM TRINIDAD

Shivanee Ramlochan
Everyone Knows I am a Haunting
ISBN: 9781845233631; pp. 72; pub. 2017; price £8.99.

Ramlochan's poetry slays whoever would force an 'identity' on it. It alchemizes the roles of grandmothers, abortionists, labourers, clerks, dancers, policemen, cousins, rapists into the greatest intensity of human. The world fucked the Caribbean archipelago, where European-derived shepherdesses and pre-Abrahamic Lilith now wander as peers among manifold beings. The music is consonantal, full of pleasure/pain. Rich as a García Márquez novel, these are uncompromising conversations, intimacy wrestling survival.

—Vahni Capildeo, author of *Measures of Expatriation*.

This debut book is a subversive tour-de-force... These stunning poems fiercely and inventively wrestle language of beast, wolf, fishtail, and gods monstrous, singing firesongs of purification for the island dead and survival for the living. In these pages of *la sangre viva*, "spirit does linger."

— Loretta Collins Klobah, author of *The Twelve-Foot Neon Woman*.

These poems crackle with soucouyant ire and the voices of duennes in stanzas so bewitching you will not want to look away... Surprise awaits in tightly wrought lines that are "no accidental shrine" to ancestry, femininity, and filial devotion. Always some darkness casts shadows against the beauty of love. Always the ghost of a story beckons the reader close.

— Rajiv Mohabir, author of *The Cowherd's Son and The Taxidermist's Cut*.

In transgressive mode, Shivanee Ramlochan invokes gods, goddesses or demons to do what poetry should do—alarm and ignite us, surprise and blast us and tear at our heartstrings. Welcome to a challenging, unforgettable and courageous new voice.

— Olive Senior, author of *The Pain Tree*.

Nicholas Laughlin
The Strange Years of My Life
ISBN: 9781845232924; pp. 72; pub. 2015; price, £8.99

The troupe of "friends" and "strangers" whom the reader meets in these poems are sometimes alter egos, sometimes aliases, sometimes adversaries. Located in worlds such as those of French film noir, spy movies, and travellers' tales, they inhabit a milieu of mistaken identity, deliberate disguise and random encounters in hotels. For the voyager, "there are too many wrong countries" and "already no one remembers you at home."

Despite the book's title, these poems are rarely autobiographical – though the tastes they reveal are intriguing – and they have few straightforward stories to tell. They are subtly humorous at one turn, sinister at another, heartbroken at the next. They puzzle over accidents, coincidences, and moments of passion, as they edge towards a sense of the world's curious strangeness, the complications of history and the encounters brought by the geography of migration.

Andre Bagoo
Pitch Lake
ISBN: 9781845233532; pp. 105; pub. 2017; price, £8.99

To look again at Bagoo's language is to realise that those poems with historic and domestic locations (some now thought of as tourist destinations) are gateways into familiarity with stranger places. ... Bagoo himself has been one of the moving spirits of the Douen Islands creative collaborators, who do not fear the douens, but re-value the shady playfulness of those childlike, voracious forest beings. This is another link between Bagoo and Caribbean contemporaries such as Shivanee Ramlochan, who are part of a new era of boundary-crossers. Under such guidance as *Pitch Lake*'s poems offer, intense strangeness sneaks up onto readers, or precipitates itself onto them...

In *Pitch Lake*, Andre Bagoo, author of the Bocas prize shortlisted poetry collection, *Burn*, displays a continuing commitment to exploration and experiment.

— Vahni Capildeo, *Newsday T & T*